K. CONNORS

Computer programming for beginners

Learn How to Code Step by Step

Copyright © 2024 by K. Connors

All rights reserved. No part of this publication may be reproduced, stored or transmitted in any form or by any means, electronic, mechanical, photocopying, recording, scanning, or otherwise without written permission from the publisher. It is illegal to copy this book, post it to a website, or distribute it by any other means without permission.

First edition

*This book was professionally typeset on Reedsy.
Find out more at reedsy.com*

Contents

Introduction	1
Chapter 1: What is Programming?	7
Chapter 2: Setting Up Your Programming Environment	13
Chapter 3: Programming Basics – Your First Steps	19
Chapter 4: Control Structures – Making Decisions in Code	26
Chapter 5: Introduction to Programming Languages	32
Chapter 6: Functions and Modular Programming	39
Chapter 7: Working with Data – Arrays, Lists, and More	46
Chapter 8: Debugging and Error Handling	53
Chapter 9: Object-Oriented Programming (OOP)	60
Chapter 10: Advanced Programming Concepts	68
Conclusion	76

Introduction

Learning to program can feel like stepping into a foreign land where everyone speaks a language you've never heard of. There's a reason why those first few steps often seem overwhelming. You're not just learning a new skill; you're learning a new way of thinking. Code is logic, distilled and refined, and for many, that's a tough pill to swallow initially. But here's the good news: If you've picked up this book, you've already started the journey, and trust me, you're in for an incredible ride.

So, what exactly is programming? To put it simply, programming is the process of giving instructions to a computer to perform specific tasks. These instructions are written in a programming language, which, just like human languages, have their own rules, grammar, and vocabulary. The magic happens when these instructions are executed, and you see the computer perform a task that you, yes you, have commanded it to do. It's a bit like being a wizard, except instead of casting spells, you're writing lines of code.

Now, let's take a step back. Computers, as we know them, are essentially dumb machines. They can't think, reason, or make decisions on their own. What they can do, however, is follow instructions with mind-blowing precision and speed. And that's where programming comes in. By writing code, you're essentially telling the computer exactly what to do, how to do it, and when to do it. The computer follows these instructions to the letter, without question, and that's why programming is such a powerful tool.

But before we dive deeper into the mechanics of programming, let's talk about why you should learn to code in the first place. In today's world, technology is everywhere. It's in your pocket, on your wrist, in your car, and even in your home appliances. And at the heart of all this technology is code. Learning to program gives you the ability to create your own technology, whether it's a website, a mobile app, or even a robot. It's like having a superpower that allows you to shape the digital world around you.

But the benefits of learning to code go beyond just being able to build cool things. Programming teaches you how to think. It forces you to break down complex problems into smaller, more manageable pieces and then solve them step by step. This kind of logical, analytical thinking is a valuable skill that can be applied to almost any area of life, from business to science to everyday problem-solving. So even if you don't end up becoming a professional programmer, the skills you'll gain from learning to code will serve you well in whatever career you choose.

Now, let's get down to the nitty-gritty of what you can expect as you embark on your coding journey. First and foremost, it's important to understand that learning to code is a process. It's not something you're going to master overnight, and that's okay. The key is to be patient with yourself and to take it one step at a time. Start with the basics, and as you become more comfortable, gradually move on to more advanced topics. Don't be afraid to make mistakes along the way. In fact, mistakes are a crucial part of the learning process. Each time you encounter an error and figure out how to fix it, you're building your problem-solving skills and becoming a better programmer.

Speaking of errors, let's talk about debugging. Debugging is the process of finding and fixing errors in your code. It's something that every programmer, from beginners to experts, has to deal with on a regular basis. In fact, some might argue that debugging is half the battle when it comes to programming. But here's the thing: Debugging isn't just about fixing mistakes. It's also about understanding how your code works and why it doesn't work the way you expected. When you debug your code, you're essentially reverse-engineering your own thought process, which can be incredibly enlightening. So instead of getting frustrated when you encounter an error, try to see it as an opportunity to learn and grow.

Another important aspect of programming is choosing the right programming language. There are literally hundreds of programming languages out there, each with its own strengths and weaknesses. Some languages are better suited for certain tasks than others, so it's important to choose the right tool for the job. For example, if you're interested in web development, you might want to learn HTML, CSS, and JavaScript. If you're more into data analysis, Python or R might be a better fit. And if you're interested in building mobile apps, Swift or Kotlin might be the way to go. The good news is that once you learn one programming language, picking up another one becomes much easier. That's because many programming languages share common concepts and structures, so the more you learn, the easier it becomes to learn even more.

One of the most common misconceptions about programming is that you need to be a math genius to be good at it. While it's true that some areas of programming, like algorithm design and data science, do require a solid understanding of math, the reality is that most programming tasks don't require advanced math skills. In fact, many successful programmers have backgrounds in fields like art, music, and literature, where math isn't typically a focus. What's more important than math skills is the ability to think logically and systematically. As long as you can break down a problem into smaller pieces and figure out how to solve each piece step by step, you'll do just fine.

Another key to becoming a successful programmer is understanding the importance of writing clean, readable code. When you're just starting out, it can be tempting to write code that works, even if it's a bit messy or hard to understand. But as you gain more experience, you'll realize that writing clean code is crucial for a number of reasons. For one, clean code is easier to read and understand, which makes it easier to debug and maintain. It's also easier to share with others, whether it's a colleague, a client, or even your future self. Trust me, there's nothing worse than coming back to a piece of code you wrote six months ago and not being able to figure out what it does because it's a tangled mess of confusing logic. So do yourself a favor and get into the habit of writing clean, readable code from the start.

But what exactly does clean code look like? For starters, it's well-organized and easy to follow. It uses meaningful variable and function names, so you can tell at a glance what each part of the code is doing. It's also well-documented, with comments that explain the purpose of each section of code and how it works. And perhaps most importantly, it's concise. Good code gets the job done with as few lines as possible, without being overly complicated. Remember, code is meant to be read by humans as well as machines, so make it as easy to understand as possible.

Finally, let's talk about the importance of practice. Like any skill, learning to code takes time and effort. The more you practice, the better you'll get. And the best way to practice is by building real projects. Start with something small, like a simple website or a basic calculator, and gradually work your way up to more complex projects. Not only will this give you a chance to apply what you've learned, but it will also help you build a portfolio of work that you can show to potential employers or clients. And don't be afraid to share your work with others. Join online communities, participate in coding challenges, and collaborate with other programmers. The more you put yourself out there, the more you'll learn, and the faster you'll improve.

Learning to code is a journey, and like any journey, it's going to have its ups and downs. There will be moments of frustration, but there will also be moments of triumph when you finally get that piece of code to work the way you want it to. And those moments of triumph, no matter how small, are what make it all worth it. So take it one step at a time, be patient with yourself, and most importantly, have fun with it. After all, programming isn't just a skill; it's a creative outlet, a way to bring your ideas to life and share them with the world. And that, my friend, is a truly amazing thing.

Chapter 1: What is Programming?

Programming is a word that gets thrown around a lot these days. It's become synonymous with all things tech, and you can hardly go a day without hearing about some new programming language, tool, or app that's changing the world. But before diving into the how of programming, it's essential to grasp the what. What exactly is programming, and why does it matter so much?

At its core, programming is about solving problems. It's the process of taking a problem or a task and creating a set of instructions that a computer can follow to achieve a desired outcome. These instructions are written in what we call a programming language, a specially designed language that computers understand. Unlike human languages, which are often ambiguous and full of nuances, programming languages are precise and unambiguous. They have strict rules about how instructions must be written, and they don't tolerate any deviations from those rules. If you write something that doesn't conform to the language's rules, the computer will simply refuse to run it, often throwing up a bunch of error messages to let you know where you went wrong.

Programming, therefore, is as much about following the rules of a particular language as it is about solving the problem at hand. But that's just the technical side of things. On a more fundamental level, programming is about logic and creativity. It's about breaking down complex problems into smaller, more manageable parts and then figuring out how to solve each part in a way that the computer can understand. And while computers might be incredibly fast and powerful, they're not particularly smart. They only do exactly what you tell them to do, nothing more, nothing less. So it's up to you, the programmer, to ensure that your instructions are clear, correct, and complete.

This brings us to the concept of algorithms. An algorithm is a step-by-step procedure for solving a problem or performing a task. It's the backbone of programming, the blueprint that guides your code. Think of it like a recipe in cooking. A recipe gives you a list of ingredients and a series of steps to follow to make a dish. An algorithm does the same thing, but instead of ingredients, you have data, and instead of steps, you have instructions that manipulate that data in some way.

For example, let's say you're writing a program to sort a list of numbers. The algorithm you use might involve comparing each pair of numbers and swapping them if they're in the wrong order, repeating this process until the entire list is sorted. This is a simple example, but the basic principle applies to much more complex tasks as well. Whether you're writing a program to calculate the trajectory of a rocket or to recommend movies on a streaming platform, you'll be following an algorithm that breaks the task down into manageable steps.

Now, programming isn't just about writing algorithms. It's also about managing data. Data is the raw material that your programs work with. It's the information that you feed into your algorithms, the stuff that gets manipulated, sorted, stored, and retrieved. In many ways, programming is all about data. How you structure it, how you access it, how you transform it—all of these are fundamental to writing good code.

When it comes to data, one of the most important concepts to understand is that of variables. A variable is like a storage container that holds a value. This value can be anything—an integer, a string of text, a list of items, or even more complex data structures. Variables are essential because they allow your programs to work with data in a dynamic and flexible way. You can change the value stored in a variable, pass it around to different parts of your program, or even use it to control the flow of your program.

Speaking of control flow, let's talk about control structures. Control structures are the building blocks of any program. They're the mechanisms that allow your program to make decisions, repeat actions, and branch off in different directions based on certain conditions. The most common control structures are conditionals and loops.

Conditionals allow your program to make decisions. For example, you might write a conditional statement that tells your program to do one thing if a certain condition is true and something else if that condition is false. This is where the "if-then-else" structure comes into play. It's like giving your program a set of instructions along with a decision-making capability. If the data looks like this, do that; otherwise, do something different.

Loops, on the other hand, are all about repetition. They allow your program to repeat a certain action over and over again until a specific condition is met. Loops are incredibly powerful because they let you automate repetitive tasks. Instead of writing out the same set of instructions multiple times, you can write them once and then loop over them as many times as necessary.

Control structures, variables, and algorithms form the foundation of programming. But as with any skill, there's more to programming than just the basics. Once you've got a handle on the fundamentals, you'll start to encounter more complex concepts, like object-oriented programming, data structures, and design patterns. These are the tools and techniques that professional programmers use to write efficient, maintainable, and scalable code.

Object-oriented programming, or OOP for short, is a programming paradigm that's based on the concept of objects. An object is a self-contained entity that contains both data and methods, which are the functions that operate on that data. The idea behind OOP is to model real-world entities as objects in your code. For example, if you're writing a program to simulate a zoo, you might create objects to represent animals, with each object having properties like species, age, and diet, as well as methods like eat and sleep. OOP is powerful because it allows you to organize your code in a way that's intuitive, reusable, and easier to manage as your programs grow in complexity.

Data structures, on the other hand, are all about how you organize and store data in your programs. There are many different types of data structures, each with its own strengths and weaknesses. Some of the most common data structures include arrays, linked lists, stacks, queues, and trees. Choosing the right data structure for a given task is crucial because it can have a significant impact on the efficiency and performance of your program.

Design patterns are like best practices for solving common programming problems. They're proven solutions that experienced programmers have developed over time, and they can save you a lot of time and effort when faced with a similar problem. Some of the most well-known design patterns include the Singleton, Factory, and Observer patterns. Learning these patterns and understanding when to use them is an essential part of becoming a skilled programmer.

But beyond the technical details, programming is also about creativity and innovation. It's about taking an idea and turning it into something real, something that can be used and experienced by others. Programming is a craft, and like any craft, it requires practice, patience, and a willingness to learn from your mistakes. It's about finding elegant solutions to difficult problems and writing code that not only works but is also beautiful in its simplicity and clarity.

One of the most rewarding aspects of programming is the sheer sense of accomplishment that comes with creating something from nothing. Whether it's a simple script that automates a tedious task or a full-fledged application that solves a real-world problem, the satisfaction of seeing your code come to life is hard to match. It's a feeling that keeps many programmers hooked, driving them to continue learning, experimenting, and pushing the boundaries of what's possible.

Of course, programming isn't without its challenges. It can be frustrating, especially when you're stuck on a particularly tricky bug or when your code just isn't working the way you expected. But it's precisely these challenges that make programming so rewarding. Each time you overcome an obstacle, you're not just solving a problem; you're growing as a programmer. You're gaining new skills, new insights, and new ways of thinking that will serve you well in the future.

In the end, programming is about communication. It's about communicating your ideas, your solutions, and your creativity to a computer in a language that it understands. It's about bridging the gap between human thought and machine logic, and in doing so, creating something that's greater than the sum of its parts. Whether you're writing a simple script or a complex system, the essence of programming remains the same: it's about solving problems, one line of code at a time.

Chapter 2: Setting Up Your Programming Environment

Setting up your programming environment is like preparing your workspace before diving into a big project. Imagine trying to paint a masterpiece without brushes or canvas. It's possible, but it's going to be messy and frustrating. Similarly, coding without a proper environment is like navigating a forest without a map—confusing and likely to get you lost. A well-configured programming environment is your map, compass, and toolkit all rolled into one, guiding you through the dense thickets of code with ease.

To begin, you need the right hardware. Contrary to popular belief, you don't need a supercomputer to start programming. A reliable, moderately fast machine will do the job just fine. Whether you choose a Mac, Windows, or Linux machine is up to personal preference, as most programming languages and tools are available across all platforms. However, it's worth noting that certain environments, like macOS, are favored for development in particular areas, such as mobile apps for iOS. That said, don't get too hung up on your machine's specs—focus instead on how comfortable you feel working on it, because you're going to be spending a lot of time together.

Once you've got your computer sorted, it's time to think about the software. At the heart of your programming environment is the Integrated Development Environment, or IDE. An IDE is a software suite that consolidates the basic tools needed for software development into a single interface. It typically includes a source code editor, a debugger, and build automation tools. The goal of an IDE is to maximize productivity by providing tight-knit components with similar user interfaces.

Choosing the right IDE can be daunting because there are so many options out there, each with its own set of features. For beginners, a lightweight and user-friendly IDE like Visual Studio Code or Sublime Text is often the best choice. These IDEs are not only easy to use but also highly customizable. You can tailor them to your specific needs by adding extensions and plugins that support different programming languages, code linters, version control integrations, and more. Visual Studio Code, for instance, has become a favorite in the developer community for its versatility and the vibrant ecosystem of extensions available.

Next up in your programming toolkit is a version control system. If an IDE is the hammer and nails of your programming environment, then version control is the blueprint that ensures everything stays in order. Version control systems, like Git, allow you to track changes in your code over time, collaborate with others, and manage different versions of your projects. With Git, you can create branches to experiment with new features without affecting your main codebase, and merge these changes back when you're satisfied with the results. This not only helps prevent catastrophic errors but also facilitates teamwork, as multiple developers can work on the same project simultaneously without stepping on each other's toes.

Setting up Git involves a few steps, but once you've got it running, you'll wonder how you ever coded without it. You start by installing Git on your machine, which is straightforward regardless of your operating system. Once installed, you'll want to set up a repository—a directory where Git can track your files. This is as simple as navigating to your project's folder in the terminal and typing a few commands. From there, you can start tracking changes, committing updates, and pushing your code to remote repositories like GitHub or Bitbucket. These platforms provide a centralized location for your code, making it easier to share with others or access from different machines.

While Git is incredibly powerful, it does come with a bit of a learning curve, especially if you're new to version control. Don't be discouraged if it feels overwhelming at first; with practice, the commands will become second nature, and you'll come to appreciate the peace of mind that comes from knowing you can always revert to an earlier version of your code if something goes wrong.

Another essential tool in your programming environment is a terminal or command-line interface (CLI). While many beginners might shy away from the terminal, it's an incredibly powerful tool that can significantly enhance your productivity. The terminal allows you to interact with your computer's operating system at a deeper level, performing tasks like navigating file directories, running scripts, and managing software packages.

Unlike graphical user interfaces (GUIs), which require you to click through multiple menus to accomplish a task, the terminal allows you to do the same with just a few keystrokes.

Learning to use the terminal is like learning a new language. It can be intimidating at first, but once you get the hang of it, you'll find yourself relying on it more and more. Start with basic commands like 'cd' (change directory), 'ls' (list files), and 'mkdir' (make directory). As you become more comfortable, you can explore more advanced commands and scripts that automate repetitive tasks, saving you time and reducing the chance of human error.

In addition to the terminal, package managers are another powerful tool that can simplify your workflow. Package managers like 'npm' for JavaScript, 'pip' for Python, and 'Homebrew' for macOS are tools that automate the process of installing, updating, and managing software packages. These packages can include libraries, frameworks, and tools that extend the functionality of your programming environment. For example, if you're working on a JavaScript project and need a specific library to handle date and time manipulation, you can simply use 'npm install' to add it to your project with minimal effort. This not only saves time but also ensures that all the dependencies are correctly configured and up to date.

As you dive deeper into programming, you'll likely encounter the need for additional tools that cater to specific needs. For instance, if you're working on web development, you might want to set up a local server to test your code before deploying it to a live environment. Tools like XAMPP, MAMP, or Node.js can help you create a local server environment that mimics a real-world server, allowing you to see how your code will behave in production. Similarly, database management tools like MySQL Workbench or MongoDB Compass can help you visualize and manage the data your applications work with.

Another aspect of setting up your programming environment involves configuring your development workflow. Your workflow is the process you follow from writing code to testing it, debugging it, and finally deploying it. A well-optimized workflow can make you more efficient, helping you write better code in less time. One way to optimize your workflow is by using task runners and build tools like Gulp, Grunt, or Webpack. These tools automate repetitive tasks like minifying code, compiling CSS, or optimizing images, allowing you to focus on writing code instead of manually performing these tasks every time you make a change.

If you're working in a team, you'll also need to consider tools for collaboration and communication. Platforms like Slack or Microsoft Teams allow you to communicate with your team members in real-time, share files, and integrate with other tools like GitHub or Jira. Project management tools like Trello, Asana, or Jira itself can help you keep track of tasks, assign responsibilities, and monitor the progress of your projects. These tools are especially useful in agile development environments, where projects are broken down into smaller, manageable tasks that are completed in short cycles, or sprints.

Security is another critical consideration when setting up your programming environment. As a programmer, you'll be handling sensitive data, whether it's your own or your users'. Ensuring that your environment is secure is essential to protecting this data and maintaining the integrity of your code. Start by setting up a firewall and antivirus software to protect your machine from external threats. Use strong, unique passwords for all your accounts, and consider using a password manager to keep track of them. If you're working on a project that involves sensitive data, encrypt your files and use secure connections when transmitting data over the internet.

Lastly, it's important to maintain a healthy balance between customization and simplicity in your programming environment. While it can be tempting to install every plugin, extension, and tool available, this can lead to a cluttered and overwhelming workspace. Instead, focus on the essentials—those tools and configurations that genuinely improve your productivity and make coding more enjoyable. As you gain more experience, you'll naturally discover which tools work best for you and how to customize your environment to fit your workflow.

In conclusion, setting up your programming environment is the foundation of your coding journey. It's about creating a space where you can work efficiently, manage your code effectively, and focus on solving problems. With the right tools and configurations, you'll find that coding becomes less of a chore and more of a creative process, where you can bring your ideas to life with confidence and ease.

Chapter 3: Programming Basics – Your First Steps

Programming can often seem like a maze of complex concepts and cryptic symbols, but at its core, it's about telling a computer what to do in a clear and logical manner. The key to mastering programming is to start with the basics, laying a solid foundation on which you can build more advanced knowledge over time. These basics include understanding the syntax and semantics of programming languages, working with variables and data types, and getting a grasp on basic input and output operations. Let's delve into each of these elements in more detail to give you a strong start on your coding journey.

Syntax is the set of rules that defines the combinations of symbols that are considered to be correctly structured programs in a given language. It's the grammar of programming languages, dictating how you must write code for the computer to understand and execute it. Just like in human languages, where a misplaced comma or incorrect verb tense can alter the meaning of a sentence, in programming, even a tiny mistake in syntax—like a missing semicolon or an extra parenthesis—can prevent your code from running altogether. While this might seem frustrating at first, mastering syntax is a crucial step toward becoming a proficient programmer.

Each programming language has its own syntax, but many share common elements, which makes it easier to learn new languages once you've mastered one. For example, in many languages, a simple statement might end with a semicolon, and blocks of code are often enclosed in curly braces. These conventions help to organize code in a way that's both logical and readable, which is important because code is meant to be read by humans as well as machines. Writing clear, well-structured code is a sign of a good programmer, and it all starts with understanding and adhering to the rules of syntax.

Moving on from syntax, let's talk about semantics. While syntax refers to the form of your code, semantics refers to its meaning. In other words, semantics is about what your code actually does when it runs. You could write code that is syntactically correct—meaning it follows all the rules of the language—but if the semantics are wrong, your code won't do what you want it to do. For example, if you're writing a program to calculate the average of a set of numbers, and you accidentally divide by the wrong number, your code might run without errors, but it won't give you the correct result. Understanding semantics is about making sure that your code not only runs but also behaves in the way you intend.

A big part of programming involves working with data, and that's where variables and data types come in. A variable is like a container that holds a value that your program can use and manipulate. This value could be anything from a number

CHAPTER 3: PROGRAMMING BASICS – YOUR FIRST STEPS

to a piece of text, and it can change as your program runs. Variables are essential because they allow you to store data that your program can access and modify as needed. In most programming languages, you'll need to declare a variable before you can use it, specifying both its name and its data type.

Data types are classifications that tell the computer what kind of data a variable can hold. The most common data types are integers (whole numbers), floats (numbers with decimal points), strings (sequences of characters), and booleans (true or false values). Understanding data types is important because it affects how your program can use the data. For instance, you can perform mathematical operations on integers and floats, but not on strings. Trying to add two strings together would result in a concatenation (joining them together), not a mathematical addition.

Let's break down these data types a bit further. Integers are straightforward—they're the numbers you learned to count with as a child. They can be positive, negative, or zero, and they don't have decimal points. Floats, on the other hand, represent real numbers, which can include fractions. They're called floats because they have a floating decimal point, meaning the decimal can appear anywhere in the number, allowing for a wide range of values.

Strings are slightly different from numbers. They're sequences of characters, meaning they can contain letters, numbers, symbols, and spaces. Strings are often used to represent text in programs, whether it's a user's name, a message, or any other piece of textual information. Strings are usually enclosed in quotation marks to distinguish them from other data types. In many programming languages, strings can be manipulated in various ways—concatenated (joined together), split into smaller strings, or searched for specific characters or sequences.

Booleans are the simplest of the data types, representing just two values: true and false. Despite their simplicity, booleans are incredibly powerful in programming because they form the basis of logic and decision-making in your code. You'll use booleans to control the flow of your program, determining whether certain blocks of code should run based on conditions you specify.

Speaking of controlling the flow of your program, let's touch on conditionals and loops, which are essential tools for making decisions and performing repetitive tasks in your code. Conditionals allow your program to make choices based on the data it has. The most common conditional statement is the "if" statement, which checks whether a certain condition is true. If the condition is true, the program runs a specific block of code; if it's false, the program can either do nothing or run an alternative block of code.

For example, you might use an if statement to check whether a user's input matches a specific value. If it does, your program might display a congratulatory message; if it doesn't, it might prompt the user to try again. Conditionals are the foundation of logic in programming, allowing your code to react to different situations in a dynamic way.

Loops, on the other hand, are all about repetition. A loop allows your program to repeat a block of code multiple times, which is useful when you need to perform the same task over and over again. There are several types of loops, but the two most common are "for" loops and "while" loops. A for loop repeats a block of code a specific number of times, based on a counter that you define. A while loop, on the other hand, repeats a block of code as long as a certain condition remains true.

Loops are invaluable in programming because they allow you to automate repetitive tasks. For example, if you need to process a list of items, you can use a loop to iterate over the list, performing the same operation on each item in turn. This not only saves time but also reduces the chance of human error, since you don't have to write out the same code multiple times.

Now, let's discuss input and output, which are how your program interacts with the outside world. Input refers to the data that your program receives, either from the user or from another source, while output refers to the data that your program sends out, whether it's displayed on the screen, written to a file, or sent over a network.

Handling input and output is a fundamental aspect of programming because it allows your programs to be interactive and responsive. In most programming languages, you can use functions or methods to get input from the user, such as asking for their name or their age. You can then store this input in a variable and use it in your program. Similarly, you can use functions to output data, whether it's printing a message to the console, writing data to a file, or sending information to another program.

Understanding input and output is crucial for creating programs that are not only functional but also user-friendly. By carefully designing how your program handles input and output, you can ensure that it meets the needs of its users, whether they're entering data through a keyboard, clicking buttons on a screen, or interacting with your program in other ways.

Finally, as you begin to write more complex programs, you'll start to appreciate the importance of comments and documentation. Comments are pieces of text in your code that the computer ignores when it runs your program. They're there for you and other programmers to read, providing explanations, notes, or reminders about what your code does and why you wrote it a certain way.

Good comments can make a world of difference when you're trying to understand your code after taking a break, or when someone else is trying to read and modify your code. While it's important to write clear and readable code, comments provide an additional layer of clarity, helping you and others understand the logic and purpose behind your code.

Documentation, on the other hand, goes beyond comments in your code. It's about creating a comprehensive guide that explains how your program works, how to use it, and how to modify it if necessary. Documentation can be as simple as a text file with instructions or as complex as a full-fledged website with tutorials, examples, and references.

Writing good documentation is an art in itself, and it's an essential skill for any programmer who wants to create software that's easy to use and maintain. Whether you're working on a small script or a large project, taking the time to document your code will pay off in the long run, making it easier for you and others to work with your code in the future.

Programming basics might seem, well, basic, but they're the foundation upon which everything else is built. By mastering syntax, semantics, variables, data types, conditionals, loops, input and output, and documentation, you're setting yourself up for success as you move on to more advanced topics and projects. Each of these elements is a crucial piece of the programming puzzle, and as you practice and gain experience, you'll find that they become second nature, allowing you to focus on solving problems and creating amazing things with code.

Chapter 4: Control Structures – Making Decisions in Code

In the world of programming, control structures are the tools that give your code the power to make decisions, repeat actions, and react to different conditions. They're like the traffic lights of programming, directing the flow of execution based on the rules you set up. Understanding and effectively using control structures is key to writing flexible, dynamic, and efficient code. This chapter will dive deep into the different types of control structures, how they work, and why they're essential for creating sophisticated programs.

At the heart of control structures are conditional statements, often referred to simply as conditionals. These are the decision-makers in your code, the logic gates that determine which path your program should take. The most basic of these is the if statement. An if statement allows your program to check whether a certain condition is true and then execute a block of code based on that truth. If the condition is false, the program skips the block of code and moves on. This simple mechanism is the foundation of logical flow in programming.

CHAPTER 4: CONTROL STRUCTURES – MAKING DECISIONS IN CODE

Let's say you want to check if a number is positive. You can write an if statement that tests whether the number is greater than zero. If it is, you might instruct your program to print out a message saying the number is positive. If it's not, the program might do nothing at all. This is the essence of control structures—they allow your program to respond to different scenarios based on the data it encounters.

Of course, real-world scenarios are rarely as simple as a single if statement. Often, you'll need to account for multiple conditions. This is where else and else if come into play. An else statement provides an alternative path for your program to take if the initial condition is false. Going back to the positive number example, you might want your program to print out a different message if the number is not positive. The else statement allows you to handle that case.

The else if statement, on the other hand, allows you to check multiple conditions in sequence. If the first condition is false, the program will move on to the else if condition. If that's also false, it will keep checking else if conditions until it finds one that's true or it runs out of conditions to check. This structure is incredibly powerful because it lets you create complex decision-making processes in your code. For example, you might write a program that checks whether a number is positive, negative, or zero, with different actions for each scenario. The if, else if, and else statements work together to ensure that only the appropriate block of code is executed based on the number's value.

But what if you have many different values to check, and writing out multiple else if statements would be cumbersome and inefficient? This is where the switch statement comes in handy. A switch statement allows you to test a variable against a list of possible values and execute different blocks of code depending on which value the variable matches. It's like a streamlined version of multiple else if statements, making your code cleaner and easier to read.

The switch statement is particularly useful when you're dealing with a limited set of possible values, such as days of the week, types of user input, or predefined categories. Instead of writing out a long chain of if-else statements, you can use a switch statement to handle each case neatly and concisely. If none of the cases match the variable's value, you can include a default case to catch any unexpected values, ensuring that your program doesn't just fail silently.

Moving on from conditionals, let's talk about loops. Loops are the workhorses of programming, allowing you to repeat actions multiple times without writing out the same code over and over again. There are several types of loops, each with its own strengths and use cases, but the most common ones are for loops, while loops, and do-while loops.

The for loop is perhaps the most versatile and widely used loop in programming. It's typically used when you know in advance how many times you want to repeat a block of code. A for loop consists of three parts: the initialization, the condition, and the increment or decrement. The initialization sets up a counter variable, the condition checks whether the loop should continue running, and the increment or decrement modifies the counter

CHAPTER 4: CONTROL STRUCTURES – MAKING DECISIONS IN CODE

variable each time the loop runs. The loop continues executing as long as the condition is true.

For example, if you want to print out the numbers from 1 to 10, you could use a for loop to do it. The loop would start with the counter set to 1, check whether the counter is less than or equal to 10, print the current value of the counter, and then increment the counter by 1. This process would repeat until the counter reaches 11, at which point the condition becomes false, and the loop stops.

While loops are a bit different. A while loop keeps running as long as a certain condition remains true, but unlike the for loop, it doesn't have a built-in counter. Instead, the condition is typically based on the state of the data your program is working with. While loops are useful when you don't know in advance how many times you need to repeat a block of code, such as when you're reading data from a file or waiting for user input.

A classic example of a while loop is reading all the lines of a file until you reach the end. The loop would continue reading and processing each line as long as there are more lines to read. Once it reaches the end of the file, the condition becomes false, and the loop stops. While loops are powerful because they give your code the ability to adapt to different situations on the fly, making them ideal for scenarios where the number of iterations can't be predicted beforehand.

The do-while loop is similar to the while loop, but with one key difference: it always runs at least once. In a do-while loop, the condition is checked after the loop has executed its block of code, not before. This means that the code inside the loop will always run at least once, even if the condition is false from the start. Do-while loops are useful in situations where you need to ensure that a block of code runs at least once, regardless of the condition.

For instance, you might use a do-while loop to prompt a user for input and then validate that input. The loop would run the prompt and validation code at least once, and then repeat the process if the input was invalid, continuing until the user enters valid input. This ensures that the user is always prompted, even if the initial condition is not met.

Nested loops are another important concept to understand. A nested loop is simply a loop inside another loop. This can be useful when you're dealing with multidimensional data structures, such as arrays or matrices. For example, if you're working with a two-dimensional array (essentially a table of data), you might use a nested loop to iterate through each row and column, performing an action on each element.

However, while nested loops are powerful, they can also be tricky to manage, especially as the number of nested levels increases. It's easy to get lost in the logic and end up with code that's difficult to read and debug. When working with nested loops, it's important to keep track of each loop's purpose and ensure that your code is as clear and concise as possible.

Control structures don't just stop at conditionals and loops, though. Another essential tool in your programming toolkit is the break statement. The break statement allows you to exit a

CHAPTER 4: CONTROL STRUCTURES - MAKING DECISIONS IN CODE

loop early, regardless of the condition. This can be useful when you've found what you're looking for and don't need to continue looping. For example, if you're searching for a specific value in an array, you can use a break statement to stop the loop as soon as you find the value, saving time and resources.

The continue statement, on the other hand, allows you to skip the rest of the current iteration of a loop and move on to the next one. This can be useful if there's a certain condition under which you don't want to execute the remaining code in the loop but still want to continue looping. For example, you might use a continue statement to skip over any invalid data in a list, processing only the valid entries.

Control structures give your code the ability to handle a wide range of scenarios, making your programs more flexible, efficient, and powerful. By mastering these tools, you'll be able to write code that not only works but also adapts to different situations, handles unexpected input gracefully, and performs complex tasks with ease. Whether you're writing a simple script or a large-scale application, understanding and effectively using control structures is key to creating software that truly shines.

Chapter 5: Introduction to Programming Languages

Programming languages are the lifeblood of coding. They're the tools that allow you to communicate with computers, instructing them to perform tasks, solve problems, and create everything from simple scripts to complex applications. While the idea of learning a programming language might initially seem intimidating—much like picking up a new spoken language—the reality is that these languages are designed to be logical and systematic. Once you get the hang of one, you'll find that learning others becomes significantly easier.

A programming language, at its essence, is a formal language comprised of a set of instructions that produce various kinds of output. Each language has its syntax, or set of rules, that governs how instructions are written and understood by the computer. What makes programming languages unique is that they are purpose-built; different languages are optimized for different tasks. This means that the language you choose will often depend on the problem you're trying to solve.

The landscape of programming languages is vast, with each

language having its own strengths, weaknesses, and community of users. To navigate this landscape, it helps to categorize programming languages into a few broad types. These categories aren't strict, but they give you a sense of the variety of tools available to you.

First, let's discuss high-level and low-level languages. High-level languages are designed to be easy for humans to read and write. They use abstract terms and concepts that are closer to human language and further from the machine's binary code. High-level languages are generally more intuitive and require fewer lines of code to accomplish tasks. Examples include Python, Java, and Ruby. These languages manage many details for you, such as memory management, which means you can focus more on solving the problem at hand rather than on the intricacies of the machine.

Low-level languages, on the other hand, are closer to the machine's hardware and give you more control over how the computer operates. Assembly language is a prime example of a low-level language. It's highly specific to the architecture of the computer's processor and requires you to manage memory and other system resources directly. While low-level languages can be more efficient in terms of performance, they are often more challenging to learn and use because they require a deep understanding of the computer's inner workings.

Next, we can look at interpreted versus compiled languages. An interpreted language is executed line by line by an interpreter, which is a program that reads your code, translates it into machine code, and then executes it on the fly. This means you can run your code as soon as you write it, making interpreted languages great for rapid development and testing. Python, JavaScript, and PHP are examples of interpreted languages. One advantage of interpreted languages is that they are often more flexible, allowing you to change your code on the go without needing to recompile everything.

Compiled languages, in contrast, are translated into machine code by a compiler before they can be run. This compilation process takes all the code and translates it into a standalone executable program. Once compiled, this program runs directly on the machine, which often results in faster execution speeds. C, C++, and Java are well-known compiled languages. The downside is that every time you make a change to your code, you need to recompile it before you can run it again, which can slow down the development process.

The choice between an interpreted or compiled language often depends on your specific needs. If you're working on a project where performance is critical, such as game development or systems programming, a compiled language might be the way to go. But if you're building a web application or scripting small tasks, an interpreted language could provide the flexibility and speed you need during development.

Another important distinction in programming languages is between statically typed and dynamically typed languages. In statically typed languages, you must declare the type of each variable before you use it. This means that the type of the variable is known at compile time, and the compiler can catch type errors before the program runs. Java, C++, and Swift are examples of statically typed languages. This approach can lead to more robust and error-free code, but it also requires more upfront effort since you need to define your types explicitly.

Dynamically typed languages, on the other hand, determine the type of a variable at runtime. This means you don't need to declare variable types explicitly; the interpreter figures it out on the fly based on the value you assign to the variable. Python, JavaScript, and Ruby are examples of dynamically typed languages. The advantage of dynamic typing is that it allows for more flexible and concise code, which can speed up development. However, this flexibility can also lead to runtime errors that would have been caught at compile time in a statically typed language.

Beyond these technical distinctions, the choice of a programming language often comes down to the specific problem domain or the environment in which you're working. Let's look at a few of the most popular languages and their typical use cases.

Python is often touted as one of the best languages for beginners due to its readability and simplicity. It uses a clear, straightforward syntax that allows new programmers to grasp the basics without getting bogged down by unnecessary complexity. Python is a general-purpose language, meaning it's versatile enough for a wide range of applications, from web development and automation scripts to data analysis and machine learning. The large and active Python community also means there are countless libraries and frameworks available to extend the language's capabilities.

JavaScript, on the other hand, is the backbone of the web. It's the language of the browser, allowing you to create interactive elements on web pages. Whether you're building a simple website or a complex web application, JavaScript is essential. Over the years, JavaScript has evolved from a simple scripting language into a full-fledged programming language capable of powering everything from server-side applications (with Node.js) to mobile apps (using frameworks like React Native). Its ubiquity in web development makes it a must-learn for anyone interested in creating anything for the web.

Java is another powerhouse in the programming world, known for its portability, scalability, and robustness. One of Java's key strengths is its "write once, run anywhere" philosophy, made possible by the Java Virtual Machine (JVM), which allows Java programs to run on any device that has a JVM installed. This has made Java a popular choice for enterprise-level applications, Android app development, and large-scale systems. While Java is more verbose than some other languages, its strong typing system and object-oriented approach make it a reliable choice for building complex, mission-critical applications.

C and C++ are the grandfathers of modern programming languages, and they continue to be relevant today. C is known for its efficiency and close-to-the-metal approach, making it the language of choice for systems programming, embedded systems, and applications where performance is critical. C++ builds on C by adding object-oriented features, making it a powerful language for building everything from operating systems and browsers to games and real-time simulations. The learning curve for C and C++ is steeper than for languages

CHAPTER 5: INTRODUCTION TO PROGRAMMING LANGUAGES

like Python or JavaScript, but the deep understanding of how computers work that comes from learning these languages is invaluable.

Ruby, much like Python, is known for its simplicity and elegance. It was designed with the philosophy of making programming enjoyable for the developer. Ruby's syntax is clean and intuitive, often resembling natural language, which makes it a pleasure to work with. Ruby on Rails, a popular web application framework built on Ruby, has been instrumental in the success of many startups and small businesses due to its ability to help developers quickly build and deploy robust web applications.

Another language worth mentioning is Swift, Apple's language for iOS and macOS development. Swift was designed to be safe, fast, and expressive, with a modern syntax that is easy to learn and use. It's quickly become the language of choice for developers building apps for the Apple ecosystem, thanks to its performance and the powerful development tools provided by Apple.

Go, often referred to as Golang, is a relatively new language developed by Google. It was created to address some of the shortcomings of older languages like C and C++, particularly in terms of managing concurrency and scalability. Go is known for its simplicity, performance, and strong support for concurrent programming, making it ideal for building scalable web servers, cloud services, and networking tools.

Finally, there's Rust, a language that has gained a lot of traction in recent years for its focus on safety and performance. Rust was designed to prevent the kinds of memory-related errors that plague languages like C and C++, without sacrificing performance. It's often used in systems programming, game development, and applications where reliability and performance are critical. Rust's unique ownership model, which ensures memory safety without a garbage collector, is one of its standout features, though it can take some time to wrap your head around.

The world of programming languages is diverse and ever-evolving, with new languages and frameworks emerging regularly. As you continue your programming journey, you'll find that different languages lend themselves to different types of problems, and part of the fun is exploring and learning new languages as you go. While it's important to have a strong grasp of one or two languages, being open to learning others will make you a more versatile and capable programmer. Each language you learn not only adds another tool to your toolkit but also broadens your understanding of programming concepts and paradigms, making it easier to pick up new languages in the future.

Chapter 6: Functions and Modular Programming

Functions are one of the most fundamental building blocks in programming. They are the tools that allow you to encapsulate a piece of logic or a specific task into a reusable block of code, making your programs more organized, efficient, and easier to understand. At their core, functions enable you to break down complex problems into smaller, more manageable pieces. This approach, known as modular programming, is key to writing clean, maintainable code.

A function is essentially a named sequence of statements that performs a specific operation or returns a value. Once you define a function, you can call it whenever you need to execute that block of code, without having to rewrite it each time. This not only saves time but also reduces the likelihood of errors since you're reusing the same, tested logic. Functions are like the building blocks of a Lego set; you can snap them together in various ways to build something larger and more complex.

To define a function, you typically start with a keyword that indicates you're creating a function, followed by a name that describes what the function does. The function's name is crucial because it should clearly communicate the purpose of the function. After the name, you list any parameters the function might need inside parentheses. These parameters act like placeholders for the data that the function will process. Finally, the function's code is enclosed within curly braces or indented, depending on the programming language. This block of code is what the function will execute when it's called.

For example, let's say you're writing a program that needs to calculate the area of a rectangle in several places. Instead of writing the same formula over and over again, you can define a function called 'calculateRectangleArea'. This function would take two parameters—'width' and 'height'—and return the product of these two values. With this function in place, whenever you need to calculate the area of a rectangle, you simply call 'calculateRectangleArea' and pass in the appropriate width and height. The function does the heavy lifting for you, and your code remains clean and concise.

One of the great things about functions is that they can return values. When a function returns a value, it sends the result of its operations back to the part of the program that called it. This allows you to use the output of a function in other calculations, assign it to a variable, or even pass it as an argument to another function. Returning values is what makes functions so powerful and versatile, as it allows them to interact with the rest of your code in meaningful ways.

In addition to returning values, functions can also modify the state of the program by changing the values of variables or

CHAPTER 6: FUNCTIONS AND MODULAR PROGRAMMING

data structures. This is often referred to as having side effects. While side effects can be useful, they can also make your code harder to reason about, especially in larger programs. To avoid unintended consequences, it's generally a good practice to keep functions as pure as possible—meaning they should focus on taking inputs and returning outputs without altering the state of the program unless absolutely necessary.

Parameters are another important aspect of functions. When you define a function, you can specify one or more parameters that the function will use in its calculations or operations. These parameters act as inputs to the function, allowing it to process different data each time it's called. Parameters make functions flexible and reusable, as they enable you to pass in different values and get different results.

There are two main types of parameters: positional and keyword. Positional parameters are the most common and must be passed in the correct order when calling the function. Keyword parameters, on the other hand, are passed by name, allowing you to specify which value corresponds to which parameter, regardless of the order. This can make your function calls clearer and easier to understand, especially when dealing with functions that have many parameters.

In some programming languages, you can also define default values for parameters. This means that if you don't provide a value for a parameter when calling the function, the function will use the default value instead. Default parameters can be incredibly useful when you want to allow for flexibility in your function calls without requiring the caller to specify every single argument.

Another powerful feature of functions is that they can be nested. This means you can define a function inside another function. Nested functions can be useful for encapsulating logic that's only relevant within the scope of the outer function. They also allow you to create closures—a concept where a nested function remembers the environment in which it was created, even after the outer function has finished executing. Closures can be a bit tricky to understand at first, but they're a powerful tool for creating more dynamic and flexible code.

Now, let's talk about scope. Scope refers to the context in which a variable or function is accessible. In most programming languages, variables defined inside a function are local to that function, meaning they can't be accessed outside of it. This is known as local scope. Local scope is important because it helps prevent naming conflicts and keeps your code modular. Variables defined outside of any function, on the other hand, are said to have global scope and can be accessed from anywhere in your program. While global variables can be convenient, they can also lead to issues with state management, so it's generally best to limit their use.

In addition to local and global scope, some languages also have block scope. Block scope limits the visibility of variables to the block of code in which they're defined, such as inside a loop or an if statement. This can help make your code more predictable and easier to debug by reducing the number of variables that are accessible at any given time.

CHAPTER 6: FUNCTIONS AND MODULAR PROGRAMMING

Functions aren't just useful for simplifying your code—they're also a key part of making your code modular. Modular programming is the practice of breaking down your code into smaller, independent modules, each responsible for a specific part of the overall functionality. By dividing your program into modules, you make it easier to manage, understand, and maintain. Each module can be developed, tested, and debugged independently, which can significantly speed up the development process and reduce the likelihood of errors.

When you write a program using modular programming principles, you typically organize your code into separate files, each containing one or more related functions. These files, or modules, can then be imported and used in other parts of your program. This not only makes your code more organized but also promotes code reuse, as you can easily share and reuse modules across different projects.

Modular programming also encourages the use of libraries and frameworks. Libraries are collections of pre-written functions and modules that provide specific functionality, such as handling dates, performing mathematical calculations, or interacting with web services. By using libraries, you can leverage the work of others and avoid reinventing the wheel. Frameworks take this concept a step further by providing a structured foundation for building entire applications, often including predefined modules, libraries, and tools to streamline the development process.

Another advantage of modular programming is that it makes it easier to collaborate with others. When working on a large project, different team members can be responsible for different modules, each focusing on their area of expertise. This division of labor not only speeds up development but also makes it easier to integrate and test the different parts of the program. And because each module is self-contained, changes to one module are less likely to cause issues in other parts of the code.

One of the best practices in modular programming is to keep your functions small and focused. A function should ideally do one thing and do it well. This makes it easier to understand, test, and reuse. If you find that a function is getting too large or trying to do too many things, it's usually a sign that it should be broken down into smaller, more specific functions. This approach, often referred to as the Single Responsibility Principle, is a cornerstone of good programming design.

When writing modular code, it's also important to think about how your modules interact with each other. You'll often need to pass data between modules, which can be done through function parameters and return values. However, it's important to keep these interactions as simple and predictable as possible. Avoid creating complex dependencies between modules, as this can make your code harder to understand and maintain. Instead, try to design your modules so that they can be easily tested in isolation, without relying too heavily on other parts of the program.

Testing is another critical aspect of modular programming. Because each module is self-contained, you can test it independently from the rest of your program. This makes it easier to identify and fix bugs before they become larger issues. Unit testing, a type of testing that focuses on individual functions and modules, is particularly well-suited to modular programming. By writing unit tests for each module, you can ensure that they work as expected and catch any regressions if changes are made later on.

Documentation is also key when working with functions and modular programming. While your code should be as self-explanatory as possible, it's still important to provide clear documentation for each function and module, explaining what it does, what parameters it takes, and what it returns. This not only helps others understand your code but also serves as a useful reference for yourself when you revisit the code in the future.

As you continue to develop your programming skills, you'll find that functions and modular programming become second nature. They're essential tools for writing code that is efficient, maintainable, and easy to understand. By breaking down your code into small, focused functions and organizing them into modules, you'll be able to tackle even the most complex programming challenges with confidence. Whether you're working on a simple script or a large-scale application, the principles of functions and modular programming will guide you in creating software that is both powerful and elegant.

Chapter 7: Working with Data - Arrays, Lists, and More

Data is the fuel that drives the engine of programming. Without data, all the code in the world would be just a bunch of lifeless instructions with nothing to act upon. The true power of programming emerges when you can store, manipulate, and retrieve data efficiently. This is where data structures like arrays, lists, and more come into play. These structures are the backbone of any program that handles information, providing the framework for storing and organizing data in ways that make it accessible and useful.

An array is one of the simplest and most fundamental data structures. At its core, an array is a collection of elements, all of which are of the same data type, stored in contiguous memory locations. What makes arrays so powerful is their ability to store multiple values under a single variable name, with each value being accessible by its index or position within the array. This allows for efficient data retrieval and manipulation, making arrays a go-to choice for many programming tasks.

Arrays are particularly useful when you need to store a fixed

CHAPTER 7: WORKING WITH DATA - ARRAYS, LISTS, AND MORE

number of elements. For example, if you're working with a set of test scores, an array can hold all the scores, allowing you to easily access, modify, or perform calculations on them. The fact that arrays are indexed means you can quickly access any element in constant time—just provide the index, and the array gives you the value. This makes operations like searching, sorting, and iterating through data much faster and more efficient.

However, arrays do have their limitations. Since they are fixed in size, you need to know the number of elements in advance. This can be restrictive in situations where the amount of data isn't predetermined. Additionally, because arrays store elements in contiguous memory, inserting or deleting elements can be costly in terms of performance. If you need to insert a new element in the middle of an array, you'll need to shift all the subsequent elements to make space, which can be time-consuming for large arrays.

This is where more flexible data structures like lists come into play. Unlike arrays, lists are dynamic and can grow or shrink in size as needed. This flexibility makes lists ideal for situations where the amount of data is variable or unknown ahead of time. Lists can store elements of different data types, though in practice, they are often used to store elements of the same type for consistency.

A list is an ordered collection of elements, similar to an array, but with a key difference: you can easily add, remove, or modify elements without worrying about the underlying memory allocation. In many programming languages, lists are implemented as linked lists, where each element, or node, contains the value and a reference to the next node in the sequence. This structure allows for efficient insertion and deletion of elements, especially when dealing with large datasets.

One of the most common operations performed on lists is iteration, where you loop through each element and perform some action, such as calculating a sum, applying a function, or checking for a condition. Iteration is straightforward with lists, thanks to their sequential nature, and is often more intuitive than with arrays, especially when dealing with varying sizes.

Beyond arrays and lists, there are other data structures designed for more specialized tasks. For instance, dictionaries (also known as hash maps or associative arrays) are another powerful data structure that allows you to store key-value pairs. Unlike arrays and lists, which are indexed by position, dictionaries are indexed by unique keys. This makes them ideal for situations where you need to associate data with a specific identifier.

For example, in a contact management application, you could use a dictionary to store phone numbers, with each contact's name serving as the key. The beauty of dictionaries lies in their ability to provide constant-time access to values based on their keys. This means that no matter how large the dictionary grows, retrieving a value by its key remains fast and efficient.

Dictionaries are incredibly versatile and are used in a wide range of applications, from storing configuration settings and user preferences to implementing caches and look-up tables. However, they also have some limitations, such as the inability to store duplicate keys and the fact that they do not maintain the

CHAPTER 7: WORKING WITH DATA - ARRAYS, LISTS, AND MORE

order of elements, which may be important in some use cases.

Another essential data structure is the stack. A stack is a collection of elements that follows the Last In, First Out (LIFO) principle. This means that the last element added to the stack is the first one to be removed. Stacks are used in many situations where a specific order of operations is required, such as undo functionality in text editors, backtracking algorithms, and parsing expressions in compilers.

Stacks are often implemented using arrays or linked lists, and they typically support two main operations: push (adding an element to the top of the stack) and pop (removing the top element). While stacks are simple, their utility in programming cannot be overstated. They provide a straightforward way to manage data that needs to be processed in reverse order, which is a common requirement in many algorithms.

Queues are another fundamental data structure, similar to stacks but with a different order of operations. A queue follows the First In, First Out (FIFO) principle, meaning the first element added is the first one to be removed. Queues are used in a variety of scenarios, such as managing tasks in a printer spooler, scheduling processes in an operating system, and handling requests in web servers.

Like stacks, queues can be implemented using arrays or linked lists. They typically support two main operations: enqueue (adding an element to the end of the queue) and dequeue (removing the front element). Queues are essential in situations where order matters, particularly when tasks or data need to be processed sequentially in the order they were received.

Beyond these basic data structures, there are more complex ones designed for specific tasks and optimizations. Trees, for instance, are hierarchical data structures that consist of nodes connected by edges. The most common type of tree is the binary tree, where each node has at most two children. Trees are used in a wide range of applications, from representing hierarchical relationships (like a family tree) to managing sorted data efficiently.

One of the most powerful types of binary trees is the binary search tree (BST). In a BST, each node has a value, and the left child's value is less than the parent's value, while the right child's value is greater. This property allows for efficient searching, insertion, and deletion operations, all of which can be performed in logarithmic time. BSTs are widely used in databases, file systems, and other applications where quick search and retrieval of data are crucial.

Another advanced data structure is the graph, which is used to represent relationships between pairs of objects. A graph consists of nodes (also called vertices) and edges that connect them. Graphs can be directed or undirected, depending on whether the edges have a direction. Graphs are incredibly versatile and are used in many applications, such as social networks, transportation networks, and dependency management in software projects.

Graphs are also the foundation of many important algorithms, such as Dijkstra's algorithm for finding the shortest path between two nodes, and the PageRank algorithm used by Google to rank web pages. Working with graphs can be complex, but they are invaluable tools for modeling and solving problems that involve relationships between entities.

As you work with these various data structures, it's important to consider the trade-offs between them. Different data structures have different strengths and weaknesses, and the choice of which one to use depends on the specific requirements of your program. For example, if you need fast access to elements by index, an array might be the best choice. If you need to store an unknown number of elements and frequently add or remove items, a list might be more suitable. If you need to associate keys with values and require fast look-up times, a dictionary could be the way to go.

Understanding the time and space complexity of each data structure is also crucial for writing efficient code. Time complexity refers to how the runtime of an operation grows with the size of the input, while space complexity refers to how much memory the data structure requires. For example, accessing an element in an array is typically an $O(1)$ operation, meaning it takes constant time regardless of the array's size. However, inserting an element into an array might be an $O(n)$ operation, where n is the size of the array, because you may need to shift other elements to make space.

By contrast, accessing an element in a linked list might be an $O(n)$ operation, because you may need to traverse the list to find the element. However, inserting an element into a linked list can be an $O(1)$ operation if you're inserting at the beginning or end, as it doesn't require shifting other elements.

Choosing the right data structure can make a significant difference in the performance of your program, especially as the size of your data grows. As you gain more experience in programming, you'll develop an intuition for which data structures to use in different situations, allowing you to write more efficient and effective code.

In conclusion, working with data is at the heart of programming, and mastering data structures like arrays, lists, dictionaries, stacks, queues, trees, and graphs is essential for any programmer. These structures provide the tools you need to store, organize, and manipulate data in ways that make your programs more powerful, efficient, and responsive to the needs of your users. Understanding the strengths and weaknesses of each data structure, as well as their time and space complexities, will enable you to make informed decisions and write code that scales gracefully as your data grows.

Chapter 8: Debugging and Error Handling

Programming is often described as a blend of art and science, and while creating elegant code that works as intended can feel like an artistic triumph, the reality is that most of the journey involves dealing with the less glamorous side of coding: debugging and error handling. Debugging is the process of identifying and fixing errors or bugs in your code, and it's something every programmer spends a significant amount of time doing. Error handling, on the other hand, involves writing code that anticipates potential issues and gracefully manages them when they occur, ensuring that your program doesn't crash unexpectedly or produce incorrect results.

Bugs are an inevitable part of programming. They can range from simple syntax errors to complex logical mistakes that cause your program to behave in unexpected ways. The first step in debugging is recognizing that there is a problem. Sometimes, this is obvious—your program might crash or produce a glaringly incorrect output. Other times, bugs are more subtle and only manifest under certain conditions or with specific inputs, making them harder to detect.

One of the most common types of bugs is the syntax error. A syntax error occurs when you write code that violates the rules of the programming language you're using. This might be as simple as a missing semicolon, an unmatched parenthesis, or a typo in a keyword. Fortunately, most modern development environments are equipped with syntax highlighting and linting tools that can catch these errors as you type, making them relatively easy to fix. The real challenge comes when you encounter logical errors—bugs that occur when your code doesn't do what you intended it to do.

Logical errors can be tricky to spot because they don't necessarily prevent your program from running; instead, they cause it to produce incorrect results. For example, you might write a loop that doesn't terminate correctly, leading to an infinite loop, or you might use the wrong operator in a calculation, resulting in incorrect output. Debugging these types of errors requires a deeper understanding of your code and the logic behind it.

One of the most effective strategies for debugging is the use of print statements. By strategically placing print statements in your code, you can track the flow of execution and see the values of variables at different points in time. This helps you identify where things start to go wrong. While print statements are a simple and accessible tool, they can become cumbersome in larger programs. This is where debuggers come into play.

A debugger is a tool that allows you to step through your code line by line, inspect the state of your variables, and even change values on the fly to see how they affect the outcome. Debuggers typically allow you to set breakpoints—specific lines in your code where the execution will pause, giving you a chance to examine the state of the program at that exact moment. This can be incredibly powerful when you're trying to track down elusive bugs that only occur under certain conditions.

Another useful technique in debugging is the process of isolation. If you suspect that a particular section of code is causing an issue, try isolating it from the rest of the program and running it independently. This can help you confirm whether the bug is located in that section and, if so, narrow down the exact line or lines responsible. Isolation can be particularly effective in larger codebases where multiple components interact in complex ways, making it difficult to pinpoint the source of a bug.

Understanding the common types of bugs and their causes can also help you debug more effectively. For example, off-by-one errors are a frequent culprit, especially in loops that iterate over arrays or lists. These errors occur when a loop runs one iteration too many or too few, often due to incorrect start or end conditions. Another common issue is null reference errors, which happen when your code tries to access an object or variable that hasn't been initialized or has been set to null. Being aware of these and other common pitfalls can help you recognize and fix them more quickly.

Once you've identified and fixed a bug, it's important to understand why it happened in the first place. This involves going beyond the symptoms of the bug to uncover the underlying cause. Maybe a variable was inadvertently modified by another part of the code, or perhaps there was a misunderstanding about how a particular function should behave. By digging deeper and understanding the root cause, you can prevent similar bugs from occurring in the future.

In addition to fixing bugs, it's crucial to write code that can handle errors gracefully. This is where error handling comes into play. Error handling is the practice of anticipating potential problems and writing code that can deal with them in a controlled manner, rather than letting the program crash or produce incorrect results. Good error handling not only makes your program more robust but also improves the user experience by providing meaningful feedback when something goes wrong.

One of the most common methods of error handling is the use of try-catch (or try-except) blocks. A try block is a section of code where you expect that something might go wrong. If an error occurs within the try block, the program jumps to the corresponding catch block, where you can handle the error—whether that means logging it, providing a default value, or notifying the user. This allows your program to recover from the error and continue running, rather than crashing.

Error handling can be as simple or as complex as your application requires. In some cases, it might be enough to catch a specific type of error, such as a division by zero, and handle it appropriately. In more complex applications, you might need to define custom error classes that encapsulate specific types of errors, allowing you to handle them in a more granular way. For example, a web application might have custom errors for different HTTP status codes, each with its own handling logic.

Another important aspect of error handling is validation. Validation involves checking that inputs to your program meet certain criteria before processing them. This can prevent many errors from occurring in the first place. For instance, if your program requires a user to enter a number, you should validate that the input is indeed a number and within an acceptable range before attempting to use it. By catching invalid inputs early, you can avoid more serious errors down the line.

It's also important to consider the user's perspective when handling errors. Users don't want to see cryptic error messages that they don't understand. Instead, provide clear, user-friendly messages that explain what went wrong and what the user can do to fix it. If possible, offer suggestions or default actions that can help the user recover from the error without needing to restart the program or lose their work.

Logging is another critical component of error handling. When an error occurs, it's important to log the details so that you can investigate later. This is especially important in production environments, where you might not have direct access to the running program. Logs can provide valuable insights into what went wrong, when it happened, and under what conditions, helping you diagnose and fix the issue more effectively. Logging can also help you identify patterns in errors, allowing you to address systemic issues that might not be apparent from a single incident.

It's worth noting that error handling isn't just about dealing with unexpected problems; it's also about designing your code to be resilient and fault-tolerant. This means thinking about what could go wrong and writing code that can gracefully handle those situations. For example, if your program depends on an external resource, such as a file or a network connection, you should consider what happens if that resource is unavailable. Rather than crashing, your program might retry the operation, use a cached version of the data, or notify the user and offer alternative actions.

Testing is another crucial part of both debugging and error handling. By writing tests for your code, you can catch many bugs and edge cases before they make it into production. Unit tests, which test individual functions or modules, can help you ensure that each part of your code behaves as expected. Integration tests, which test how different parts of your application work together, can help you catch issues that might arise from interactions between components. And finally, end-to-end tests, which simulate user interactions with your application, can help you ensure that the entire system works as intended.

Writing tests also forces you to think about how your code handles different scenarios, including edge cases and error conditions. This can lead to better-designed code that is more resilient and easier to debug. Moreover, having a solid test suite can give you confidence when making changes to your codebase, as you can quickly verify that your changes haven't introduced new bugs.

As you gain more experience in programming, you'll develop a toolkit of debugging and error-handling strategies that work best for you. Whether it's setting up strategic breakpoints, using advanced logging techniques, or writing thorough tests, these skills will become second nature. Debugging and error handling are integral parts of the programming process, and mastering them is key to becoming a skilled and effective programmer.

By embracing these challenges and learning to navigate the complexities of debugging and error handling, you'll not only improve the quality of your code but also gain a deeper understanding of how your programs work. This understanding will serve you well as you tackle more complex projects and continue to grow as a developer. Debugging isn't just about fixing mistakes; it's about learning from them and using that knowledge to write better, more reliable code. And in the end, that's what programming is all about—continuously improving, learning, and building something that works, even when things don't go as planned.

Chapter 9: Object-Oriented Programming (OOP)

Object-Oriented Programming, often abbreviated as OOP, is one of those concepts in programming that can feel like a bit of a buzzword when you're first starting out. But don't let the jargon fool you—OOP is a powerful and practical paradigm that can make your code more organized, reusable, and easier to manage. At its core, OOP is about modeling real-world entities as objects within your code, and then defining the interactions between these objects to create complex systems. By the time you're done reading this chapter, you'll have a solid understanding of how OOP works, why it's so useful, and how to apply it to your programming projects.

To begin with, let's talk about what exactly an object is in the context of OOP. An object is a self-contained unit that contains both data (often referred to as attributes or properties) and methods (which are functions that operate on the data). Think of an object as a blueprint that combines both what something is and what it can do. For instance, if you were writing a program to manage a library, you might have an object representing a book. This book object would have properties like the title, author, and

CHAPTER 9: OBJECT-ORIENTED PROGRAMMING (OOP)

ISBN, and methods like borrow and return.

One of the key principles of OOP is encapsulation. Encapsulation is the idea that an object's internal state—its data—should be hidden from the outside world, and only accessible through well-defined methods. This is like having a control panel on a machine; you can push buttons and turn dials to interact with the machine, but you don't need to see or understand all the gears and wires inside to make it work. Encapsulation helps to protect the integrity of an object's data by preventing external code from directly modifying it in ways that could lead to inconsistencies or errors.

Another fundamental concept in OOP is inheritance. Inheritance allows you to create new classes (a class is a blueprint for creating objects) that are based on existing ones, inheriting their attributes and methods while also introducing new features or modifying existing ones. This is a powerful way to reuse code and create hierarchies of related objects. For example, in your library program, you might have a base class called Item, which represents any item in the library. The Item class could have properties like title and publication date, and methods like checkOut and returnItem. From this base class, you could create more specific classes like Book, Magazine, and DVD, each inheriting the common properties and methods from Item, but also adding their own specific features.

Polymorphism is another cornerstone of OOP. It's a fancy word that means "many forms," and in programming, it refers to the ability of different objects to respond to the same method in different ways. Polymorphism allows you to write more flexible and general code. Going back to the library example, let's say you have a method called printDetails that's meant to display information about an item. Thanks to polymorphism, you can define printDetails in the base Item class, but then override it in each subclass to display the specific details relevant to a book, magazine, or DVD. When you call printDetails on an object, the correct version of the method is automatically used, depending on the type of object you're dealing with. This makes your code more adaptable and easier to maintain.

The fourth pillar of OOP is abstraction. Abstraction is all about reducing complexity by hiding unnecessary details and exposing only the relevant parts of an object's functionality. It's closely related to encapsulation but goes a step further by simplifying the interface of an object. For example, you don't need to know how a book's due date is calculated when you borrow it; you just need to know that you can call the borrow method and the due date will be set automatically. By abstracting away the complexity, you make your code easier to use and understand.

Classes, as mentioned earlier, are the blueprints from which objects are created. When you define a class, you're essentially setting up a template that describes what properties and methods the objects created from this class will have. Once you have a class, you can create multiple instances of it, each of which is a separate object with its own state. For example, using your Book class, you could create several book objects, each representing a different book in the library. While these objects share the same structure, each one has its own unique data, such as a different title or author.

CHAPTER 9: OBJECT-ORIENTED PROGRAMMING (OOP)

In most OOP languages, classes can include constructors, which are special methods that are automatically called when an object is created. Constructors are typically used to initialize an object's properties, ensuring that it starts out in a valid state. For instance, when you create a new book object, the constructor might require you to provide the title, author, and ISBN, so that the object is fully set up and ready to use from the moment it's created.

Methods within a class can be categorized as instance methods or class methods. Instance methods operate on a specific instance of a class, meaning they can access and modify the data specific to that object. For example, the borrow method would be an instance method, since it affects the state of a particular book object. Class methods, on the other hand, operate on the class itself rather than on individual objects. These methods can be used for tasks that are related to the class as a whole, rather than to any one object. For instance, you might have a class method that keeps track of the total number of books in the library.

Another important concept in OOP is the idea of composition. While inheritance allows you to create new classes by extending existing ones, composition lets you build more complex objects by combining simpler ones. Composition is often described with the phrase "has-a" rather than "is-a." For example, instead of creating a subclass for a special kind of book that has an audio version, you might have a Book object that "has an" AudioFile object as one of its properties. This approach allows for more flexibility and can help avoid some of the pitfalls of deep inheritance hierarchies, such as increased complexity and reduced reusability.

When designing a system using OOP principles, one of the challenges is deciding how to structure your classes and objects in a way that makes sense for the problem you're trying to solve. This often involves identifying the key entities in your system and figuring out how they relate to each other. These relationships can be modeled using inheritance, composition, or a combination of both. It's important to strike a balance between generality and specificity—create classes that are general enough to be reusable but specific enough to capture the details of the domain you're working in.

Encapsulation, inheritance, polymorphism, and abstraction are sometimes referred to as the four pillars of OOP, and for good reason. Together, these principles provide a framework for building software that is modular, reusable, and easier to maintain. By breaking down complex systems into smaller, self-contained objects, OOP allows you to manage the complexity of software development more effectively.

One of the benefits of OOP is that it aligns well with the way we naturally think about the world. We tend to categorize things into classes and think about their attributes and behaviors. This makes OOP an intuitive way to model real-world problems in software. For example, in a simulation game, you might have objects representing different types of characters, each with their own attributes like health, strength, and intelligence, and methods like move, attack, and heal. These objects can interact with each other in ways that mirror real-world interactions, making the game more realistic and engaging.

OOP also encourages the use of design patterns—standard solutions to common problems in software design. Design patterns provide a way to structure your code in a way that is both efficient and understandable. For example, the Singleton pattern ensures that a class has only one instance and provides a global point of access to it. This can be useful in situations where you need to coordinate actions across a system, such as managing connections to a database.

The Factory pattern, another common design pattern in OOP, involves creating objects without specifying the exact class of the object that will be created. This is particularly useful when the type of object to be created is determined at runtime based on certain conditions. The Factory pattern helps to decouple the code that creates objects from the code that uses them, making your code more flexible and easier to extend.

OOP isn't without its criticisms, though. Some argue that it can lead to overly complex hierarchies and tangled dependencies if not used carefully. Others point out that the flexibility of OOP can sometimes result in slower performance compared to more procedural or functional programming approaches. However, when used appropriately, OOP remains one of the most effective ways to manage complexity in large software projects.

Another aspect of OOP that's worth mentioning is the concept of interfaces and abstract classes. An interface is a contract that defines a set of methods that a class must implement, without providing the actual implementation. Abstract classes, on the other hand, can provide some implementation but are intended to be extended by other classes. These concepts are useful for defining common behaviors across different classes without forcing them into a rigid hierarchy.

For instance, in a drawing application, you might have an interface called Drawable with methods like draw and resize. Different shapes, such as circles and rectangles, would implement this interface, each providing its own version of the draw and resize methods. This allows you to treat different shapes in a uniform way, even though their implementations might be very different.

Abstract classes are similar but can include both abstract methods (which must be implemented by subclasses) and concrete methods (which are already implemented). They are useful when you have some common functionality that you want to share among multiple subclasses but still need to enforce certain methods to be implemented by each subclass.

OOP also plays nicely with testing and debugging. Because objects are self-contained units of code, they can be tested in isolation from the rest of the system. This makes it easier to write unit tests, which are tests that check the functionality of individual components. By testing objects independently, you can catch bugs early and ensure that each part of your system works correctly before integrating them into the larger application.

When it comes to debugging, OOP's modularity also pays off. If something goes wrong, you can often trace the issue back to a specific object or method, making it easier to identify and fix the problem. Encapsulation ensures that changes to one part of the system don't inadvertently affect others, reducing the likelihood of introducing new bugs when making updates.

As you continue to explore OOP, you'll find that it offers a powerful way to think about and solve problems in software development. By organizing your code into objects and using the principles of encapsulation, inheritance, polymorphism, and abstraction, you can build systems that are robust, flexible, and easier to maintain. OOP may take some time to master, but once you get the hang of it, it becomes an invaluable tool in your programming toolkit. Whether you're working on a small project or a large-scale application, the principles of OOP will help you create code that is not only functional but also elegant and easy to understand.

Chapter 10: Advanced Programming Concepts

As you delve deeper into the world of programming, you'll eventually encounter advanced concepts that can significantly enhance your ability to write efficient, maintainable, and scalable code. These concepts go beyond the basics of syntax, control structures, and basic data handling, diving into areas that allow you to tackle more complex problems and optimize your solutions. In this chapter, we'll explore some of these advanced topics, including recursion, concurrency, design patterns, and memory management. Each of these areas can profoundly impact how you approach coding and the types of solutions you can craft.

Let's begin with recursion, a concept that, while often seen as a bit daunting at first, becomes incredibly powerful once understood. Recursion is a method of solving problems where a function calls itself as a subroutine. This might sound like it could quickly spiral out of control, but when implemented correctly, recursion allows you to break down complex problems into smaller, more manageable pieces. Recursion is particularly useful for problems that can be naturally divided into similar

CHAPTER 10: ADVANCED PROGRAMMING CONCEPTS

subproblems, such as searching through a tree structure, sorting algorithms like quicksort or mergesort, and even solving puzzles like the famous Towers of Hanoi.

In a recursive function, there are two key components: the base case and the recursive case. The base case is the condition that stops the recursion—essentially, it's the simplest version of the problem that can be solved without further recursion. The recursive case is where the function calls itself with a modified version of the original problem, gradually working towards the base case. Without a proper base case, a recursive function would continue to call itself indefinitely, leading to a stack overflow error as the program runs out of memory to keep track of all the function calls.

One of the challenges with recursion is ensuring that each recursive call brings you closer to the base case, avoiding infinite loops. It's also important to consider the performance implications of recursion, particularly the potential for stack overflow in languages that don't optimize tail recursion. In some cases, iterative solutions (using loops) can be more efficient, but recursion often provides a more elegant and straightforward approach, especially for problems that have a naturally recursive structure.

Next, let's discuss concurrency, a concept that becomes increasingly important as you work with more complex and performance-critical applications. Concurrency refers to the ability of a program to execute multiple tasks simultaneously, or at least manage multiple tasks in a way that makes it appear they are happening simultaneously. This is crucial in modern computing, where applications often need to handle multiple inputs or processes at once, such as responding to user interactions, processing data, and communicating with external services.

There are several models of concurrency, including threading, multiprocessing, and asynchronous programming. Threading involves running multiple threads of execution within the same program, allowing tasks to be performed in parallel. Each thread shares the same memory space, which makes communication between threads easy but also introduces the possibility of conflicts, known as race conditions, where two threads try to modify the same piece of data at the same time. Properly managing access to shared resources, typically through the use of locks or other synchronization mechanisms, is crucial to avoiding these issues.

Multiprocessing, on the other hand, involves running multiple processes, each with its own memory space. This approach avoids the pitfalls of shared memory but can involve more overhead due to the need for inter-process communication. Multiprocessing is particularly useful for CPU-bound tasks that can be distributed across multiple cores to improve performance.

Asynchronous programming, often seen in event-driven systems and modern web applications, is another approach to concurrency. It involves writing code that can perform other tasks while waiting for an operation to complete, such as waiting for data from a network request. Asynchronous programming allows your program to remain responsive even when dealing with potentially slow operations, by using callbacks, promises,

CHAPTER 10: ADVANCED PROGRAMMING CONCEPTS

or async/await constructs to handle tasks without blocking the main thread of execution.

Concurrency introduces complexity into your code, requiring careful consideration of how tasks are managed and how data is shared between them. However, mastering concurrency can greatly enhance the performance and responsiveness of your applications, particularly in environments where handling multiple tasks simultaneously is critical.

Another advanced concept that plays a significant role in writing clean, efficient code is the use of design patterns. Design patterns are standard solutions to common problems in software design, distilled from the experience of many developers over the years. They provide a template for how to structure your code in a way that is both effective and maintainable. While design patterns aren't a one-size-fits-all solution, they offer valuable guidance when faced with recurring design challenges.

One of the most well-known design patterns is the Singleton pattern, which ensures that a class has only one instance and provides a global point of access to that instance. This can be useful for managing resources like a database connection or a configuration manager, where having multiple instances could lead to conflicts or inconsistent states.

Another common pattern is the Observer pattern, which is used to establish a one-to-many dependency between objects so that when one object changes state, all its dependents are notified and updated automatically. This is particularly useful in scenarios like GUI applications, where changes in the model need to be reflected in the view, or in event-driven systems where various components need to react to certain events.

The Factory pattern is another important design pattern, especially in object-oriented programming. It provides an interface for creating objects but allows subclasses to alter the type of objects that will be created. This is particularly useful in situations where your code needs to be flexible and scalable, enabling the creation of objects without specifying the exact class of the object that will be created. The Factory pattern promotes loose coupling in your code, making it easier to extend and maintain.

The Decorator pattern is used to extend the functionality of objects in a flexible and reusable way. Instead of modifying the original object, decorators wrap it with additional functionality, which can be stacked or composed in different ways. This pattern is particularly useful when you need to add responsibilities to objects dynamically, such as adding logging, caching, or authentication layers in a web application.

Moving on to memory management, this is another advanced area that can have a significant impact on the performance and stability of your programs. Memory management involves the efficient allocation, use, and release of memory during a program's execution. In many programming languages, memory management is handled automatically by a process known as garbage collection, which periodically scans for and frees up memory that is no longer in use.

However, understanding how memory management works

CHAPTER 10: ADVANCED PROGRAMMING CONCEPTS

under the hood can help you write more efficient code and avoid common pitfalls, such as memory leaks and excessive memory consumption. A memory leak occurs when a program allocates memory but fails to release it after it's no longer needed, leading to a gradual increase in memory usage over time. If left unchecked, memory leaks can cause a program to consume all available memory, leading to crashes or degraded performance.

In languages that don't have automatic garbage collection, such as C and C++, memory management is entirely manual, requiring you to allocate and free memory explicitly. This gives you more control over memory usage but also introduces the potential for errors, such as dangling pointers (references to memory that has already been freed) or double freeing (attempting to free memory that has already been released). Mastering manual memory management requires a deep understanding of how your program interacts with the underlying hardware and the discipline to follow best practices for memory allocation and deallocation.

Even in languages with garbage collection, understanding how memory allocation works can help you optimize your code. For instance, frequent allocation and deallocation of small objects can lead to fragmentation, where the memory is divided into many small, non-contiguous blocks, making it difficult to allocate larger blocks of memory. This can result in performance issues, particularly in programs that need to handle large amounts of data or run for extended periods.

To mitigate these issues, you can use techniques such as object pooling, where a pool of objects is pre-allocated and reused instead of being repeatedly created and destroyed. This approach can reduce the overhead associated with memory allocation and improve the performance of your program.

Another important aspect of memory management is understanding the difference between stack and heap memory. The stack is a region of memory that stores local variables and function call information. It is managed automatically, with memory being allocated and deallocated as functions are called and return. The stack is fast and efficient but limited in size, making it unsuitable for large or long-lived data.

The heap, on the other hand, is a region of memory used for dynamic allocation, where memory is allocated and deallocated manually or by the garbage collector. The heap is larger and more flexible than the stack but also slower and more prone to fragmentation. Understanding when to use stack versus heap memory, and how to manage heap memory effectively, is crucial for writing high-performance programs.

Lastly, let's touch on the concept of algorithms and data structures, which are the bedrock of efficient programming. An algorithm is a step-by-step procedure for solving a problem, and the choice of algorithm can have a huge impact on the performance of your program. Common algorithms include sorting algorithms (like quicksort and mergesort), searching algorithms (like binary search), and graph algorithms (like Dijkstra's shortest path algorithm).

Choosing the right algorithm involves understanding the trade-

CHAPTER 10: ADVANCED PROGRAMMING CONCEPTS

offs between time complexity (how fast the algorithm runs) and space complexity (how much memory the algorithm uses). For example, a quicksort might be faster than a bubblesort for large datasets, but it also requires more memory. Understanding these trade-offs allows you to choose the most appropriate algorithm for your specific problem.

Similarly, the choice of data structure can significantly impact the efficiency of your program. For example, using a hash map for quick lookups can be much faster than searching through a list, especially as the size of the dataset grows. Knowing when to use a stack, queue, linked list, tree, or graph can help you organize your data in a way that optimizes performance and simplifies your code.

Understanding advanced programming concepts like recursion, concurrency, design patterns, memory management, and algorithms opens up new possibilities in how you approach problem-solving in code. These concepts allow you to write more efficient, scalable, and maintainable programs, taking your skills as a programmer to the next level.

Conclusion

As you navigate the world of programming, it's easy to get caught up in the sheer complexity and vastness of the field. From the first time you wrote a simple "Hello, World!" program to diving deep into object-oriented programming, memory management, and advanced algorithms, the journey can sometimes feel overwhelming. Yet, this journey is precisely what makes programming such a rewarding endeavor. It's not just about writing code that works; it's about crafting solutions, solving problems, and continuously evolving your skills.

One of the most significant realizations you might have as you progress is that programming is not just a technical skill but also a mindset. The ability to break down complex problems into manageable pieces, to think logically about how to structure your code, and to anticipate and handle potential issues are all part of this mindset. As you've seen throughout this book, programming requires more than just knowing the syntax of a language. It's about understanding the principles that underpin how computers work and how you can best leverage those principles to achieve your goals.

CONCLUSION

At the heart of programming is the concept of problem-solving. Whether you're building a simple script to automate a repetitive task or developing a full-fledged application that will be used by thousands of people, you're always solving problems. Sometimes these problems are straightforward, like finding a bug in your code or optimizing a slow function. Other times, they're more abstract, such as designing a system that can scale to handle millions of users or architecting a complex algorithm that can process vast amounts of data efficiently. Regardless of the nature of the problem, the satisfaction that comes from finding a solution is one of the great joys of programming.

But let's not romanticize it too much—programming can be tough. There are days when nothing seems to work, when you're stuck on a bug that just won't go away, or when the complexity of the project at hand feels insurmountable. These moments of frustration are as much a part of the process as the moments of triumph. The key is perseverance. Every programmer, no matter how experienced, faces challenges and setbacks. What sets successful programmers apart is their ability to keep pushing forward, to keep learning, and to keep refining their skills.

Learning to program is like learning a new language, except this language gives you the power to create. With every new concept you master—whether it's control structures, functions, or object-oriented design—you're adding tools to your toolkit. And just like with any craft, the more tools you have and the more proficient you become in using them, the more creative and effective you can be in your work.

One of the most rewarding aspects of programming is seeing

your code come to life. Whether it's a small script that saves you hours of manual work each week or a full-blown application that people rely on daily, there's something incredibly satisfying about creating something from nothing. This sense of creation, of turning ideas into reality, is what drives many people to become programmers in the first place. And as you've likely experienced, it's a feeling that never really gets old.

But programming is not just about the code you write—it's also about the community you become a part of. The programming community is vast and diverse, full of people who are passionate about solving problems and building cool stuff. Whether you're contributing to open-source projects, participating in coding competitions, or just asking questions on forums, you're joining a global network of individuals who share your interests and challenges. This community can be a tremendous resource, providing support, feedback, and inspiration as you continue to grow as a programmer.

Another important aspect of programming is the constant evolution of technology. The tools, languages, and frameworks you use today might be different from what you'll be using five or ten years from now. This rapid pace of change can be daunting, but it's also what makes programming so exciting. There's always something new to learn, whether it's a new programming paradigm, a more efficient algorithm, or a tool that makes development faster and easier. Embracing this constant learning is essential to staying relevant and effective as a programmer.

As you've worked through the various topics covered in this

book, you've likely noticed how interconnected different programming concepts are. Understanding data structures, for example, is crucial when designing algorithms, which in turn is essential when writing efficient code. Object-oriented programming provides a framework for organizing your code, making it easier to manage and extend, while knowledge of memory management helps you optimize your programs for performance. Each concept builds on the others, creating a solid foundation that you can continue to expand as you take on more complex challenges.

Another key aspect of programming is the balance between theory and practice. While it's important to understand the underlying principles of computer science, it's equally important to get hands-on experience by writing code, building projects, and solving real-world problems. Theoretical knowledge gives you the foundation you need, but practical experience is what turns that knowledge into skill. It's through the act of coding—through trial and error, debugging, and iteration—that you truly internalize what you've learned.

One of the more subtle, yet crucial, lessons in programming is the importance of writing clean, readable code. Code isn't just written for machines to execute—it's written for other programmers (and your future self) to read and understand. As you've learned, writing clear, well-documented code can save you a lot of headaches down the road. It's the difference between code that works and code that's maintainable, scalable, and easy to debug. As you continue to develop your skills, you'll find that the time you invest in writing clean code pays off in spades when it comes to maintaining and expanding your projects.

Programming also teaches you to think critically and analytically. It sharpens your problem-solving skills and encourages you to approach challenges from different angles. When you encounter a bug or a tricky algorithm, you learn to break down the problem, consider various solutions, and evaluate their trade-offs. This way of thinking extends beyond the world of code—it's a skill that's valuable in virtually every aspect of life.

In the broader context, programming is a gateway to endless possibilities. With coding skills, you can create apps, automate tasks, analyze data, build websites, and so much more. The versatility of programming means that it can be applied to virtually any field, from finance to healthcare to entertainment. This flexibility allows you to combine your programming skills with your other interests, opening up a wide range of career opportunities and personal projects.

The landscape of programming is always expanding, with new languages, frameworks, and technologies emerging all the time. This constant evolution means that there's always something new to learn, whether you're a beginner or a seasoned professional. Staying curious and open to learning new things is one of the most valuable traits a programmer can have. It's this curiosity that drives innovation and keeps the field of programming vibrant and dynamic.

While it's important to stay up-to-date with the latest trends and tools, it's also worth remembering that the core principles of programming don't change. Concepts like algorithms, data structures, and design patterns are foundational, and mastering them will serve you well no matter what new technologies come along. By focusing on these fundamentals, you build a strong base that will support you as you explore new areas and take on more complex challenges.

As you continue on your programming journey, you'll likely encounter moments of frustration and doubt—times when a bug seems insurmountable or a concept feels just out of reach. But these moments are all part of the process. Every programmer has faced them, and every programmer has overcome them by continuing to learn, experiment, and practice. It's through these challenges that you grow as a programmer, developing not just your technical skills, but also your resilience and problem-solving abilities.

Programming is as much about creativity as it is about logic. It's about finding innovative solutions to problems, experimenting with new ideas, and pushing the boundaries of what's possible. Whether you're designing a user interface, optimizing an algorithm, or building a new feature, programming gives you the tools to turn your ideas into reality. And that's what makes it so rewarding—it's a craft that allows you to create, to build, and to bring your visions to life.

In the end, programming is a journey of continuous learning and growth. It's a journey that challenges you to think deeply, to solve problems creatively, and to constantly improve your skills. The knowledge and experience you gain along the way are invaluable, not just for your career, but for your personal development as well. Programming teaches you to think critically, to approach challenges with confidence, and to embrace the power of technology to make a difference in the world.

Printed in Great Britain
by Amazon